C000227175

IMAGES
of England

MADE IN
BIRMINGHAM

ELECTRO AND SILVER PLATING
SKETCHED AT THE WORKS OF MESSRS. ELKINGTON AND CO., VISITED BY H.R.H. THE PRINCE OF WALES

MODELLING

GOLD PLATING

SMALL STAMP

ENTRANCE TO THE WORKS

SOLDERING

An engraving of scenes at Elkington, Mason & Co.'s pioneering electro-plating works in New Hall Street. It not only provides a (somewhat sanitised) image of a city at the forefront of the technological revolution of its time but, by commemorating a visit to the factory by the Prince of Wales, makes clear that British industry had the royal – hence, social – stamp of approval. (Fittingly, the building was later adapted as the Museum of Science & Industry.)

IMAGES
of England

MADE IN
BIRMINGHAM

Compiled by
Keith Turner

TEMPUS

First published 2001
Copyright © Keith Turner, 2001

Tempus Publishing Limited
The Mill, Brimscombe Port,
Stroud, Gloucestershire, GL5 2QG

ISBN 0 7524 2252 9

Typesetting and origination by
Tempus Publishing Limited
Printed in Great Britain by
Midway Colour Print, Wiltshire

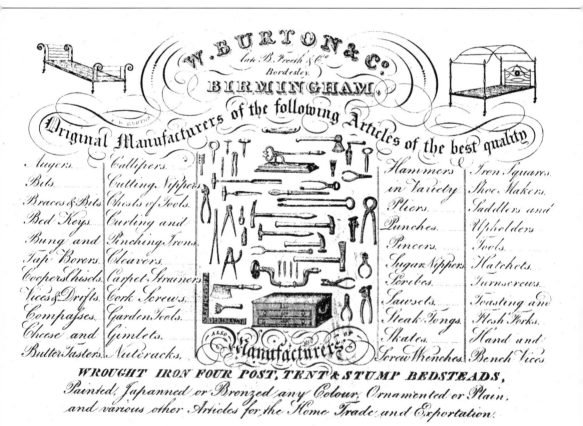

An early 1880s trade advertisement for W. Burton & Co. of Bordesley – the original centre of Birmingham's metal-bashing industries. The sheer diversity of items made is astonishing by today's standards.

Contents

Acknowledgements

I should like to thank, once again, my former colleagues in Birmingham Central Library for showing such forbearance in the face of the disruption occasioned during the compilation of this book. Grateful thanks also to Margaret for all her help with the background research. Once again, a debt of gratitude must be acknowledged to all those local photographers whose prints are gathered in the library; without their earlier endeavours this compilation would never have been possible.

Another early 1880s trade advertisement, this time for Snow Hill manufacturer B. Day's patent chimneybreast fittings of 'Portability and elegance'. The clear inference to be drawn was that no *nouveau riche* home was complete without them.

Introduction

It is difficult to condense Birmingham's manufacturing history into a volume such as this: whole tomes could be – indeed have been – written on its individual industries. And what industries they were! Think of Birmingham and a host of internationally-known brand names spring to mind: Austin cars, Avery weighing machines, BSA rifles, Cadburys chocolate, Chad Valley toys and games – and that is only the start of the alphabet.

What made this comparatively insignificant Warwickshire market town a world leader in so many products? Quite simply, the answer lay in its location. Lacking mineral resources to mine and smelt, or water in sufficient quantities to power machinery, the entrepreneurs of Birmingham had to make do with what they had if any sort of industrial base was to be built up. And what they had, in the late eighteenth and early nineteenth centuries, was access to a major transport network – what today would be termed 'infrastructure' – in the shape of the English canal system. With Birmingham ideally placed at the very centre of this waterway network, fuel and raw materials could be brought in by barge; the one could then be used to process the other and the finished goods dispatched the same way to the major textile-manufacturing towns of Yorkshire and Lancashire to the north, and to the ever-ravenous metropolis of London to the south.

So Birmingham prospered, its reputation as a manufacturing centre growing by leaps and bounds after a local craftsman's son, Matthew Boulton, built his famous Soho Manufactory in 1762 in order to produce all manner of metal objects and, when James Watt joined the concern a few years later, massive steam engines to kick-start the country's Industrial Revolution. If conditions are favourable, such growth has a momentum of its own. With sufficient supplies of cheap materials, fuel and labour, and with a growing market hungry for their products, factories will expand and prosper while ancillary industries spring up as the original factories generate their own niche markets for products such as tools and boxes. Add a host of support services such as banking, insurance, printing, laundering and public transport and before long the town is fast becoming a fully-fledged city.

First and foremost though – in industrial terms – Birmingham was a metal-bashing town. That is to say, metal in its just-refined or smelted state would be purchased from outside – often from no further afield than the Black Country immediately to the north-west – and worked by hand or machine into a saleable product, be it a brass button, a silver teapot or a motorcar. In modern parlance, the workshops and factories were 'adding value' to the raw material. That is to say, if a certain amount of metal cost £1, and it could be transformed into an object that could be sold for £5, providing the cost of effecting such a transformation in terms of rent, fuel, labour, repayment to investors and so on did not exceed £4, then that business would make a profit. And judging by their longevity, that is exactly what many of Birmingham's industries did.

Value could be added in two ways. The first was to use highly-skilled craftsmen to produce high-quality, expensive goods of which jewellery, guns and motor cars are probably the best known Birmingham products; the second way was use cheap labour and high-volume mechanical processes to churn out low-cost items such as badges, buttons, whistles and pen nibs. This was the paradox at the heart of Birmingham's manufacturing industry: high quality products were produced side by side with the cheap and cheerful 'Brummagem ware'. Both approaches are amply illustrated in the following pages.

Much of the city's industrial base fell prey in the twentieth century to competition from overseas where vast pools of cheap labour could be used to undercut the prices of many home-produced goods; further relentless pressure was applied later by the gradual 'globalization' trend of many industries – notably car manufacturing – with production being switched from one country to another at the stroke of an accountant's pen. Whatever the future holds, it seems certain that the phrase 'made in Birmingham' will never carry the same worldwide message it once did.

Keith Turner
July 2001

Two further advertisements, from the same period, for products indicative of Birmingham's new-found status as a town where almost anything and everything was made.

One
Metal Bashing

'Metal bashing' might seem a slightly derogatory phrase to outsiders, but it is one that has been used proudly in Birmingham to describe the metal-working trades at the heart of the city's industrial activity. In numerous back-street workshops – and later in purpose-built giant factories – raw metal would be cast, forged, plated, enamelled, machined, spun, turned and stamped into a thousand and one objects: some finished articles in their own right, some vital components destined to become part of larger products in other factories, both here and abroad. It is an activity that continues to this day, though by no means on its former scale.

Where Birmingham's reputation as a metal-working centre began: Boulton & Watt's Soho Manufactory in Handsworth, c. 1851. The original print is a platinotype by W. B. Osborn.

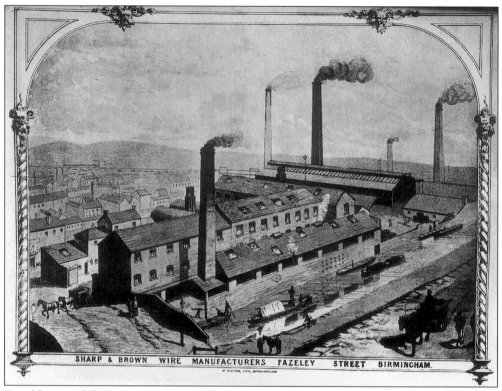

SHARP & BROWN WIRE MANUFACTURERS FAZELEY STREET BIRMINGHAM.

An old print of the premises of Messrs Sharp & Brown, wire manufacturers, in Fazeley Street. Like many nineteenth-century Birmingham factories, it is located alongside a canal for ease of unloading raw materials and loading finished products.

The Nos 118-125 Lionel Street premises of Fisher, Brown & Bayley Ltd, bedstead manufacturers, 1902. Here iron rods are being guillotined by machine to the correct length...

...before their ends are forged, by hand, to make bedstead stretchers. Astonishingly, there were nearly fifty bedstead-producing businesses in Birmingham in 1902 – indicative perhaps of its growing population and housing developments.

Still at Fisher, Brown & Bayley in 1902. Here angle irons are punched and studded...

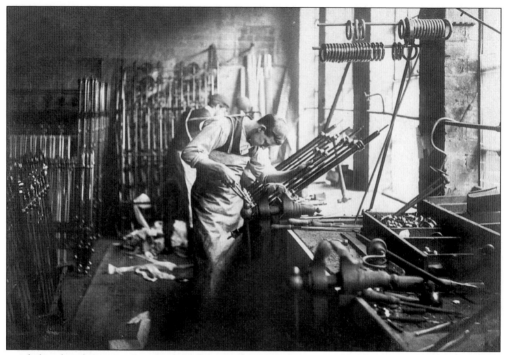

...while elsewhere in the factory brasswork trimmings are fitted to the bed-ends. Such decorative touches make surviving examples from this period desirable antiques today.

Weaving wire mattresses at the same factory, again in 1902. Unlike the more arduous metal-working, this was considered suitable employment for women.

Finally, completed bedstead parts await packing. For obvious space-saving reasons, the finished bedsteads would be dispatched to retailers in a 'knock-down' form.

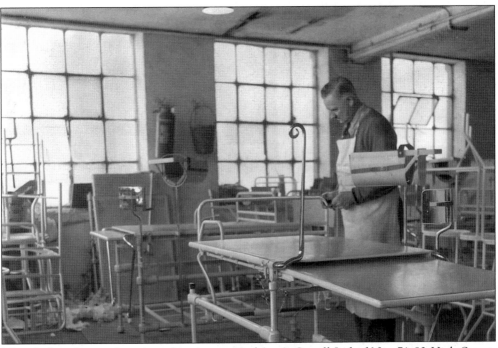

More bedstead manufacturing, this time at Hoskins & Sewell Ltd of Nos 71-83 High Street, Bordesley, probably in the 1920s. The factory conditions are a vast improvement on those at Fisher, Brown & Bayley. These 'bedsteads' are in fact patients' trolleys destined for the Civil Hospital at Khartoum in the Sudan.

Another Hoskins & Sewell product line was ship's berths. Here one is being checked; note the fold-up sides, designed to stop the occupant from falling out in rough weather!

Hoskins & Sewell also supplied four-poster bedsteads for the luxury end of the market. Here a particularly decorative iron and brass model is being assembled.

The Hooper Street, Spring Hill, workshops of the Birmingham Engineering Co. Ltd, *c.* 1910. Here parts for machine tools are being made: on the right by skilled male operatives (who would have endured a long apprenticeship) and, behind the screens in the left distance, by unskilled women.

A closer view of one of the women workers' sections of the Birmingham Engineering Co.'s factory.

Before the First World War many considered a woman's place to be in the kitchen – in this case, the Birmingham Engineering Co.'s works kitchen, *c.* 1910. But the coming conflict was to change all that.

The staff at the Alldays & Onions Pneumatic Engineering Co. Ltd of Sydenham Road and Fallows Road, on the border of Sparkbrook and Small Heath, just before the First World War. The firm specialised in manufacturing machinery for factories. The unavoidable question is: how many of these men and boys will shortly enlist – and how many will pay the ultimate price for doing so?

The Heath Street premises of Earle, Bourne & Co. Ltd, tube manufacturers, 1911. Only the solitary figure and the firm's delivery van give a human scale to the scene. This sequence of photographs is from a portfolio recording the firm's new factory.

The impressive front entrance to the office block, and a unique glimpse into a vanished industrial age.

The Boardroom. Here the directors of the company would meet to ponder matters of policy and finance.

The General Manager's Office, looking for all the world like the parlour in a middle-class home!

The Company Secretary's Office. More formal than the General Manager's, it is obviously intended as a working environment. An early electric fire stands in the hearth.

The General Office, province of clerks and typists. Whoever answered the telephone was apparently not encouraged to sit down on the job.

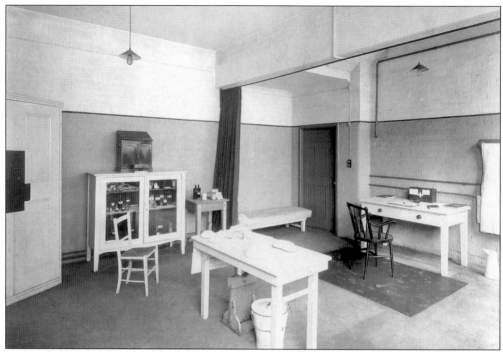

The factory's surgery. The provision of such a facility surely reflected an enlightened attitude on the part of the directors towards their workforce.

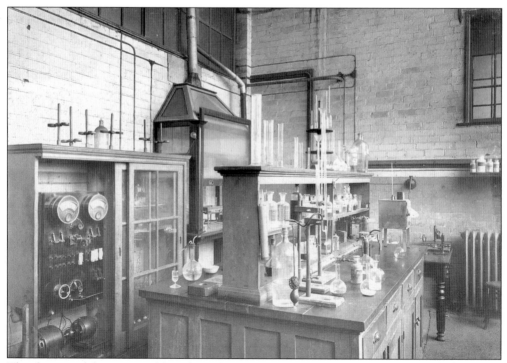

The factory's laboratory. Although undoubtedly state-of-the-art at the time, it looks like nothing so much as a school chemistry lab of some fifty years later.

Inside the factory proper. This is the Metal-inwards Warehouse where, as its name suggests, metal billets were stored after delivery.

The Metal Stores Weighing Department. Here the billets and other metal items would be weighed and sorted according to the use about to be made of them. Note that off-cuts are also stored here, presumably prior to being re-worked, or sold as scrap.

Part of the Casting Shop. This is where the factory carried out its own casting work, with complicated shapes being cast from molten metal, rather than being machined from solid with accompanying wastage of material.

Rolling Mill No. 1. Here billets of metal would be rolled into flat sheets as required.

The factory's other Rolling Mill, No. 2.

The Solid-drawn Tube Mill. This is where tubes would be manufactured, drawn out, by machine, from solid metal.

The Foremen's Mess Room. The rigid factory hierarchy of the period ensured that the holders of such posts did not have to eat with the shopfloor workers.

The Canteen Kitchen. Catering for the bulk of the workforce, this presumably also served the Foremen's Mess Room as well.

The Canteen, filled with hungry workmen – including boys well below today's school-leaving age. As with the photograph on p. 16, one wonders just how many of those here will survive the coming war.

The Roof Garden – perhaps the most socially-levelling place in the entire factory. Here men and women of all ages, and probably from a range of social backgrounds, could meet freely on fine days during breaks from their workshop and offices duties.

SPECIMEN OF TREADWAY STEEL FLOORING BY
FISHER & LUDLOW LTD. BIRMINGHAM

An undated publicity postcard from Fisher & Ludlow Ltd of the Albion Works, Rea Street. The firm pressed everything from steel-mesh industrial flooring...

STEEL FRAMED BUILDING ERECTED BY
FISHER & LUDLOW LTD., BIRMINGHAM

...to entire framed buildings!

Inside Fisher & Ludlow's pressing shop, probably around 1930. The company also manufactured car body parts and was taken over by the British Motor Corporation in 1953 (see also Chapter Five).

Spinning a paraboloid reflector from a 7ft-diameter aluminium blank for use in a radar installation, by the London Aluminium Co. Ltd, probably during the late 1940s or early 1950s. Spinning is the process of gradually forcing a rotating metal disc over a wooden former in order to produce a dish or bowl-shaped vessel.

The London Aluminium Co. Ltd, c. 1935. Producing 'Diamond' aluminium household utensils – in this instance coffee pots and kettles – at either its Westwood Road, Witton or Charles Henry Street works.

At the other end of the size scale: a stainless steel food processing plant under construction at the company's Witton works.

A complete chemical plant built by the company, principally from copper and aluminium, probably in the 1940s. The unit shown in the following photograph, or a number similar to it, would appear to have been incorporated into the plant.

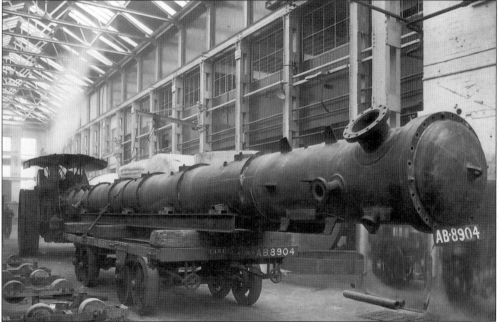

A chemical plant unit produced by the London Aluminium Co., again probably in the 1940s. It has been fabricated at the company's Bradford Street works from 'Everdur' (a copper alloy) and, at some 45ft long and 11 tons in weight, requires the services of a traction engine to move it.

The Parkinson Stove Co. Ltd, in Station Road, Stetchford, *c*. 1935. Here pre-stamped metal panels are being fed into an enamel sprayer and dryer, probably to become parts of those pastel-coloured domestic gas cookers so evocative of the period. Enamelling is the process of baking coloured glass powder onto metal in order to form an extremely durable and corrosion-proof surface.

Inside the workshops of H.E. Hazlehurst Ltd, tool makers of Nos 168-173 Darwin Street, 5 December 1958. The girls working at the machines would be engaged on relatively unskilled, routine tasks – skilled engineering still very much a male preserve at this time.

A girl sorts nibs at Perry & Co. (Pens) Ltd of No. 36 Lancaster Street, probably in the 1950s. According to the 1954 *Kelly's Directory* for Birmingham, the firm made 'every description of steel pens & penholders, stationers' sundries, stamped & pressed metal sundries'. In the days before the fountain pen, Birmingham produced two-thirds of the world's steel nibs - a total of many millions a year!

A lady cleans burners for oil lamps at Sherwoods Ltd of Granville Street. Lamp parts, like pen nibs, were relatively cheap and simple to mass-produce, and a typical example of the high-volume, low-cost side of Birmingham manufacturing.

Albion Works in Great Hampton Row, 7 July 1959. Brassfounders. This and the following three photographs record the premises of four firms providing specialist services to the city's metal-working concerns. (The service provided is either apparent from the firm's title, or has been added afterwards.)

Joseph Crossbee Ltd, Hospital Street, 7 July 1959. Casting specialists.

The Reliance Pattern Making Co. and the ETP Co. Ltd, toolmakers and machinists, Villa Street, 7 July 1959. A pattern was an exact replica, usually of wood, made so that a metal item could be cast in a mould made from it.

The Reeve Polishing & Plating Co. in Clifford Street, 7 July 1959.

In the workshops of the Birmingham Guild of Handicraft, probably around 1960. Birmingham craftsmanship at its finest: gates are being fashioned for the Royal Bank of Scotland.

A further view of the gates being assembled. The Guild was formed during the late nineteenth century by followers of the Arts & Crafts movement. It became a limited company in 1895, with premises on Great Charles Street opening in 1898.

Pitt & Swatkins Ltd, metal spinners, Nos 11-13 St Paul's Square, *c*. 1960. This is another of the specialist service firms that clustered around the fringes of the Jewellery and Gun Quarters.

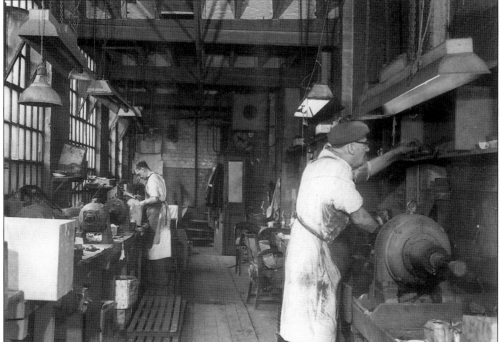

In the workshop of W.A. Humphries Ltd, at No. 45 Hockley Hill, on 16 March 1967. This was another firm of metal-spinners, again located in that north-centre area of the city referred to above.

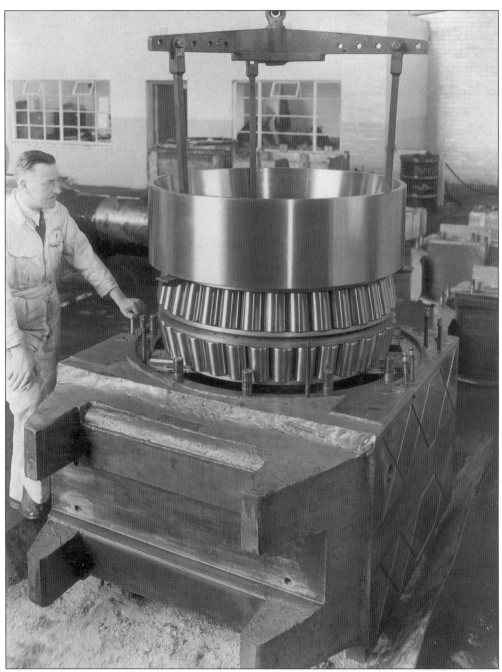

Inside the factory of ball and roller bearing manufacturer British Timkin Ltd in Cheston Road, Aston, *c.* 1960. This is a four-row, 42in diameter bearing, weighing 4,775lbs, and destined for a slabbing mill. Its massive size provides a fascinating contrast with those shown on pp 68-69.

Another Operation on a large bearing race (unidentified) at British Timkin Ltd, probably again in 1960.

A Gibbons furnace at ICI (Metals) Ltd, Birmingham. The furnace is used to heat copper billets.

Full circle: a Boulton & Watt beam engine of 1817, as used for pumping water out of mines, unveiled at Dartmouth Circus on the new Aston Expressway in 1971. Sadly, it is in a rather neglected condition today.

BEAM BLOWING ENGINE
BUILT BY BOULTON AND WATT IN 1817

PRESENTED TO THE CORPORATION BY M. & W. GRAZEBROOK LIMITED
IN WHOSE WORKS THIS ENGINE SUPPLIED AIR TO THEIR BLAST FURNACES
FOR A PERIOD OF 131 YEARS.

RE-ERECTED BY BIRMINGHAM PUBLIC WORKS DEPARTMENT.

THIS PLAQUE WAS UNVEILED BY THE PRIME MINISTER
THE RT. HON. EDWARD HEATH. M.B.E. M.P.
ON THE 30TH. SEPTEMBER, 1971

The beam engine's on-site plaque recording the unveiling.

Two
The Jewellery Trade

Side by side with the metal bashing illustrated in the previous section, Birmingham was also home to a thriving precious metal-working trade centred in the off-centre area of the city known as the Jewellery Quarter. Here tiny workshops produced anything from tiny items of personal jewellery to large pieces of silver tableware – and still do so today – while a host of other workshops provided essential support services such as tool-making, metal engraving and the manufacture of jewellery boxes. Retail outlets abound, and a former set of workshops has become a fascinating 'frozen in time' museum.

A jeweller at work. Such scenes have been a feature of Birmingham manufacturing life for well over a hundred years, altering little in that time with tools and techniques remaining comparatively unchanged. In this instance the setting is the firm of Wright & Hadgkiss Ltd of No. 9 Vyse Street.

A bird's eye view of the centre of the Jewellery Quarter, 1971. Radiating from the landmark Chamberlain clock are Frederick Street (top), Warstone Lane (left and right) and Vyse Street (bottom). The large building, centre bottom, is the Rose Villa Tavern.

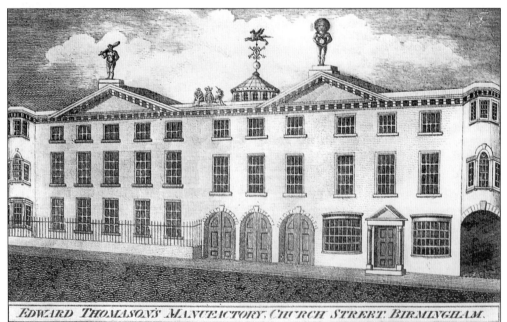

EDWARD THOMASON'S MANUFACTORY, CHURCH STREET, BIRMINGHAM.

Plate, Spoons, Forks &c.&c.	— Made —	Real and Imitation Jewellery
Plated Services w.th Silver Embossm.ts	Exclusively here the	Diamonds, Gems, Pearls,
Plated Cutlery, Spoons &c. on Steel.	PATENT	Gold & Silver Snuff Boxes
Fine Cut Glass for the Table	Carriage Step, Gun Lock	Buttons, including Livery Buttons
Bronz'd, or Molu Figures & Lustres.	Cork Screw, Sword Cane, Hearth Brush, Umbrella &c.	Gold Silver & Bronz'd Medals & Tokens

An early advertisement for Edward Thomason's Church Street firm. His impressive listed output ranges from cutlery to sword-sticks, jewellery (real and imitation) to buttons; such was the versatility of many of the jewellery trade's businesses.

Vyse Street, 1967. One of the streets at the heart of the Jewellery Quarter, virtually all premises in it are connected in some way with the trade. No. 123, for example, houses Engelhard Industries Ltd, platinum specialists.

Another stretch of Vyse Street, again in 1967. Several of the premises on the right are occupied by ring manufacturers, with a block in the centre devoted to the striking of medals and medallions.

The west side of Great Hampton Street, 1900. Although now largely confined to the area bounded by Vyse Street, Spencer Street and Warstone Lane, the Jewellery Quarter once extended rather further afield, as the signs on these Georgian houses-turned-workshops indicate.

Nos 55-56 on the east side of Great Hampton Street, 1901. No. 56 is home to S.F. Evans & Co., electro-plating specialists, while No. 55 is occupied by L.J. Meakin & Co., one of the trade's many support firms, offering a range of services from die sinking to the manufacture of craftsmen's stools, all of which helped make the Quarter virtually self-contained in such matters.

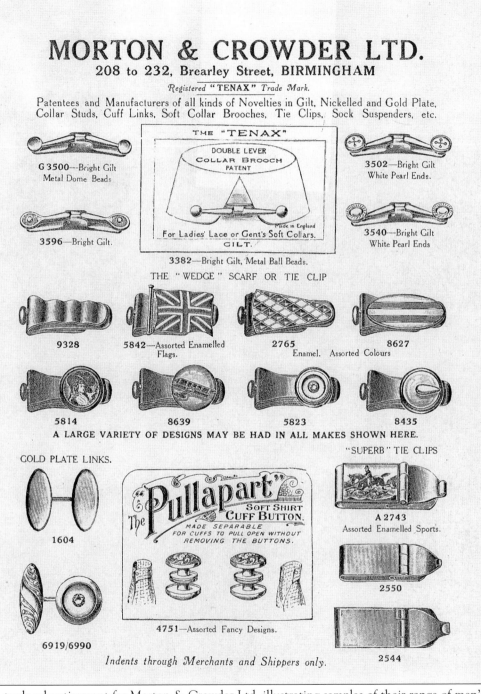

A trade advertisement for Morton & Crowder Ltd, illustrating samples of their range of men's jewellery, from the Birmingham Jewellers' & Silversmiths' Association *Buyers' Guide* for 1920. Brearley Street is off the eastern edge of what is considered the Jewellery Quarter today, being some distance beyond the other side of Great Hampton Street.

A collection of 'penny souvenirs', 1905. These had been made three years before for the coronation of King Edward VII and virtually all carry portraits of him and/or his Queen, Alexandra. This particular collection was presented to the city's Museum & Art Gallery in 1963.

William Pearsall's High Street jeweller's shop, 1900. Souvenirs such as those shown in the previous picture would no doubt have formed part of this jeweller's stock at the time of the coronation, after he had re-located to New Street. Small outlets like this often had their own workshop in the back, unlike today's high street retail chains.

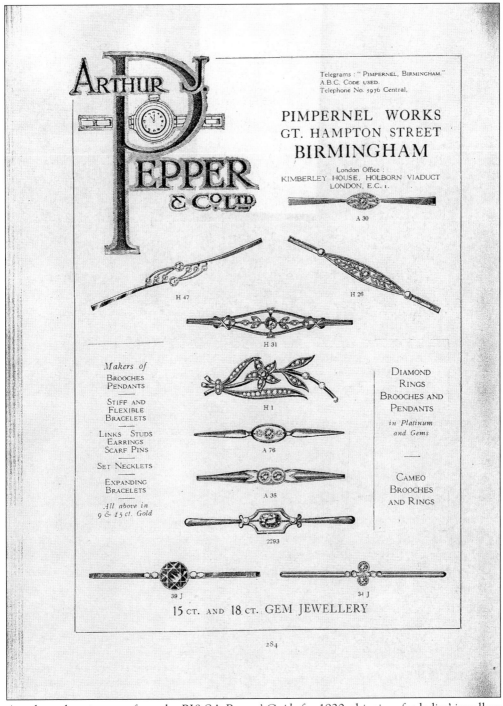

Another advertisement from the BJ&SA *Buyers' Guide* for 1920, this time for ladies' jewellery from Arthur J. Pepper & Co. Ltd of Great Hampton Street.

A workman at Sherwoods Ltd of Granville Street. He appears to be using a lathe to chase or engrave a pattern onto a piece of silverware.

Another silversmith at work, this time at the Barker Ellis Silver Co. of Unity Works on Constitution Hill. Parts of an ornate candelabra are being painstakingly manufactured and checked against the example on the bench.

A silversmith at work at Adie Bros Ltd. This is a timeless study of a craftsman at work, putting the finishing touches to a silver salver with a padded hammer and wooden workblock, probably older than he is, at the firm's Atlas Works on Soho Hill.

This and the following three photographs were taken in the same workshops as the previous one, at or around the same time, and show a variety of jewellers' tools and techniques in use. Here a workman uses a pair of pliers to hold a handle in place while it is soldered onto a presentation cup.

The blowtorch in use again, this time on a silver box – possibly intended to hold cigarettes.

Smoothing away any rough edges on a jug, with a fine file, prior to polishing.

Hammering-out defects in the base of another presentation cup, probably destined to become a winner's trophy for some future sporting event.

At Adie Bros again, this time in 1953. Here the central dish of an ornate two-foot diameter silver fruit bowl is fluted…

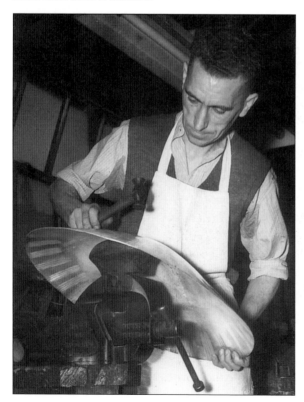

…before receiving its final surfacing. The bowl, commissioned to commemorate the coronation of Queen Elizabeth II, will be added to the city's collection of civic plate when completed.

At the Birmingham Assay Office in Newhall Street, 1952. Here Birmingham's hallmark, an anchor, is being applied to a large silver dish. Seemingly a peculiar choice for somewhere so far inland, the symbol was chosen because much of the lobbying of Parliament for an assay office was carried out in the Crown & Anchor pub in the Strand in London – the other lobbyist at the time (1773) was Sheffield, which took a crown as its mark! (A jokey reference to this event can be seen in the pavement outside the Assay Office.)

Marking a teapot, 1952. All items of precious metal – jewellery, cutlery or whatever – made in Birmingham would normally be sent to this Assay Office for marking, as a guarantee of their purity. A date letter to indicate the year would also be stamped onto the piece, in this case a capital C, of a particular font, to denote 1952. Prior to the move to Newhall Street in 1893, the Assay Office was located in Little Cannon Street.

F. & A. JOHNSTONE

MANUFACTURING

Jewellers & Diamond Mounters

71, VYSE STREET, BIRMINGHAM.

15 ct. & 9 ct. Jewellery

Telephone : Central 2957. (Code : A.B.C. (5th Edition.)

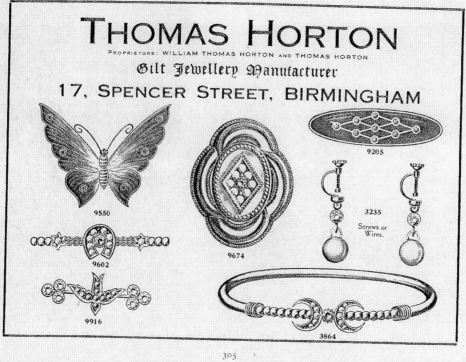

THOMAS HORTON

PROPRIETORS: WILLIAM THOMAS HORTON AND THOMAS HORTON

Gilt Jewellery Manufacturer

17, SPENCER STREET, BIRMINGHAM

9550

9205

3235
Screws or
Wires.

9602

9674

9916

3864

305

Two further advertisements to finish with, again from the BJ&SA *Buyers' Guide* for 1920. Spencer Street was then, and still is, at the very heart of the Jewellery Quarter.

Three
The Gun Trade

Close by the Jewellery Quarter, at the southern end of Constitution Hill, lies Birmingham's Gun Quarter, the focus for the manufacture of guns and rifles. Once extending from Snow Hill in the west to Lancaster Street in the east, and from the Fazeley Canal in the north to Lichfield Street (now the lower end of Corporation Street) in the south, the southern portion has been subject to much redevelopment over the years, the construction of the Inner Ring Road alone accounting for the destruction of a great swathe of properties.

A typical Birmingham gunsmith's workshop recreated by the city's Science Museum (presently closed, pending a move to new premises in Digbeth).

The corner of Bath Street and Shadwell Street, 12 August 1959. Like the Jewellery Quarter, Birmingham's Gun Quarter was crammed with tiny workshops occupying Victorian (or earlier) houses.

The showroom of William Wellington Greener, gunmaker, 1898. The contrast between the typical gunsmith's workshop and a company's showroom, where sporting gentlemen would be invited to place their order, or make their choice of purchase at leisure, could hardly have been greater. This firm had premises in No. 22 St Mary's Row and Nos 61-62 Loveday Street at this time.

Drilling the bores on two shotgun barrels at the BSA's Shirley works, probably in the 1950s. Two machines can be seen, with the stationary drills nearest the camera. The solid barrel forgings (top right) are rotated while the hollow drill bits are forced against them. Oil pumped through the drill bits by the machine in the background cools and lubricates the cutting edges.

This and the following five photographs show further stages of the gunmaking process at BSA. Here the ribs are being fitted, by hand, between the two barrels of a double-barrelled shotgun. The firm – the Birmingham Small Arms Co. Ltd – was founded in 1861 with a factory on the appropriately-named Armoury Road in Small Heath, and quickly became the largest private manufacturer of guns in Europe, before adding bicycles and motorbikes to its output.

Engraving a shotgun lock mechanism by hand.

A lock engraver at work. Using small chisels and a light hammer – or simply finger pressure – the intricate tracery design would be engraved onto the metal by eye. No pattern or guidelines would be drawn or otherwise marked out first, the engraver preferring to copy the design directly from a previously-made example.

The details of every weapon made would be recorded meticulously before it left the factory, as is being done here.

All guns would be tested as well, on the company's own indoor firing range.

Boxing the tested rifles for dispatch. In this case, they are small-bore Martini-International target rifles, a favourite model for shooting clubs and tournaments.

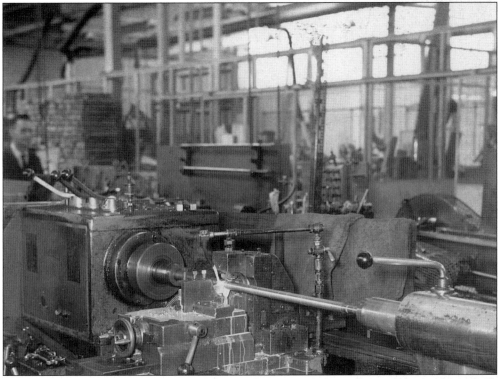

This and the following sequence of photographs were taken in the workshops of Mitchell, Bosley & Co. Ltd, and depict similar gunmaking stages, c. 1960. This is a barrel-boring machine, slightly more modern in design but similar in principle to that portrayed on p. 55.

Inspecting the bore of a small-bore barrel for any obvious flaws or defects. The firm was based in Little Shadwell Street in the Gun Quarter and specialised in the manufacture of gunstocks.

Selecting a suitable block of wood – probably walnut – from which a gunstock will be shaped. The blocks have already been machine-cut into a roughly triangular shape in readiness for hand-carving.

Wet and dry sanding of an almost-finished stock, as performed by Jack Hinsley.

Further wet and dry sanding by Mr Hinsley. Note that the trigger mechanism has now been attached.

The completed lock and stock – now waiting to receive the barrels…

…which are finally fitted.

A close-up of the underside of a double-barrelled shotgun, minus its stock.

A completed gun undergoes expert appraisal in the hands of Bill Homer. In common with many other craftsmen-centred industries, workers in the gun trade could expect to find employment for life – often with the same firm – and in the process would accumulate a wealth of experience which would tell them at once if a product was 'right' or 'wrong'.

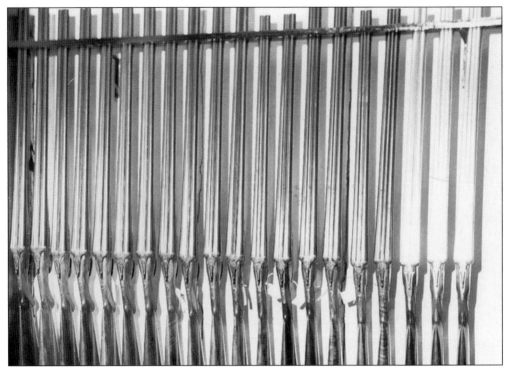

Gleaming, finished guns are racked for display and – the manufacturers hope – a quick sale.

Finally, testing a finished Mitchell, Bosley gun at the Proof House under the watchful eye of Proof Master Roger Lees. The Proof House, in Banbury Street, was opened in 1814 and acts as an assay office for the gun trade, marking weapons with the 'proof' of their quality.

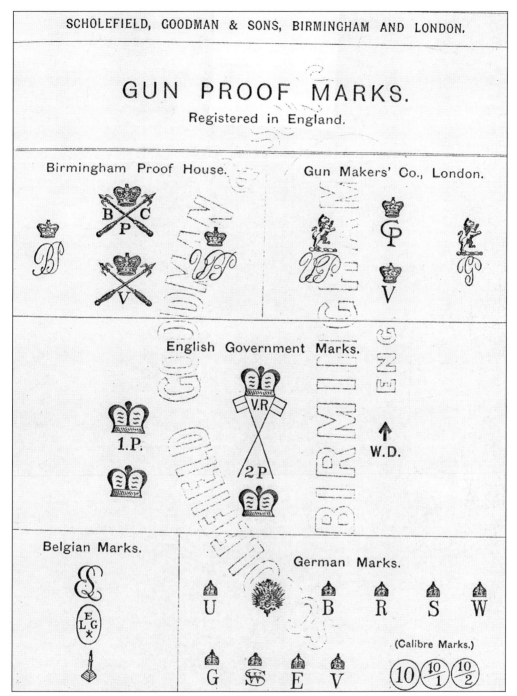

Gun proof marks, as depicted in the March 1898 catalogue of gunmakers Scholefield, Goodman & Sons of 135 Edmund Street. Those for the Birmingham Proof House are shown top left.

65

135, Edmund Street,

Birmingham,

March, 1898.

Dear Sir,

We have pleasure in handing you a New Edition of our Gun List.

We have carefully revised the prices throughout and have brought up the styles and patterns to the present date. We trust it will lead to increased orders.

Please note that **all prices are NET,** subject to the usual terms of payment, and to alteration without advice.

We are, Dear Sir,

Yours very truly,

Scholefield, Goodman & Sons.

DIRECTIONS FOR MEASURING A GUN.

Place a perfectly straight piece of wood along the barrels of gun and fill in the measurements indicated below.

A to B.....................inches.

C to D..................... ,,

E to H..................... ,,

F to H..................... ,,

G to H..................... ,,

The introduction to Scholefield, Goodman & Sons' catalogue for March 1898. The 'Directions for measuring a gun' are for the benefit of customers wishing to order further guns to the same dimensions as those previously tailor-made to suit them.

Four
War Production

Birmingham, as a major manufacturing centre, played a crucial role in the country's war effort in both the First and Second World Wars. For some firms, already established in the business of manufacturing weapons and munitions, the two wars generated an inevitably sharp rise in demand for their products. For others, their production lines were given over to the war effort – Cadburys, for example, turned from the making of chocolate (considered an unnecessary luxury item in wartime) to the manufacture of, among other things, gasmasks. Either way, such a volume of war production in Birmingham made the city a legitimate bombing target, especially during the Second World War, with devastating results. As will be seen from the photographs, large numbers of women were recruited for war production, filling jobs previously closed to them in the engineering industry – as they would be again once hostilities ceased.

Weighing artillery shell cases at an unidentified factory, sometime during the Second World War. The three men – two workhands and a works manager perhaps – are obviously posing for the camera: real production would have been a high-speed activity.

The first of four views inside an unidentified Birmingham ball bearing factory, during the First World War. This is the stockpile of differing diameter steel tubes from which the ball races will be machined.

The machined ball races are cleaned and polished. Such bearings were a vital component of many weapons, and certainly no military vehicle, ship or aircraft, could move without them.

Roller bearings being assembled and checked. As the name suggests, cylindrical steel rollers are used instead of steel balls inside the race, giving a greater distribution of the load on the bearing.

Stocks of finished bearings, of all sizes, await dispatch to other factories for incorporation into one kind of engine of destruction or another.

The Birmingham firm of W. & T. Avery Ltd, a major supplier of weighing machines to shops and factories throughout Britain, was also part of the war effort, producing machines adapted for munitions work. The central sign on this publicity float reads: 'The Avery automatic weigher for Ministry of Munitions to weigh high explosives at the rate of 30 tons per hour'.

Another Avery publicity float – again, probably in a parade to help the war effort – this time featuring its Parnell catering equipment subsidiary. A reminder that all those workers and soldiers had to be fed!

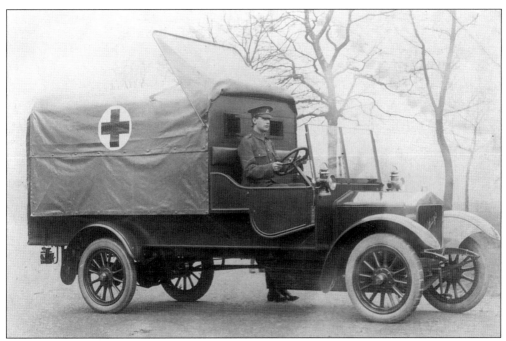

A First World War field ambulance produced by Alldays & Onions, pneumatic engineers (see also p. 16). The vehicle appears to be an adaptation of a lengthened motor car, make unknown but badged as Alldays on the radiator grill.

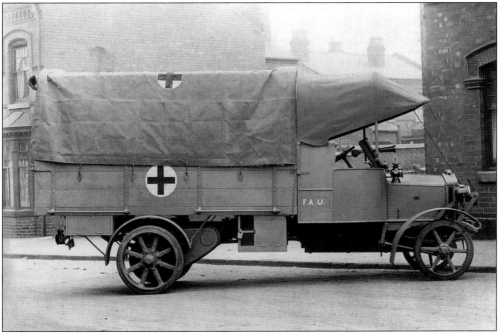

Another Alldays & Onions ambulance, this time based on a lorry chassis. Note the enclosed chain-drive to the rear axle, and high mudguards, for work in the appalling conditions on the Western Front. (Other Alldays & Onions vehicles are illustrated in the *Birmingham Transport* volume in this series.)

Another First World War sequence, this time depicting the production of Mills Munitions Ltd's instantly-recognisable hand grenades. Here the cast-metal bodies of the grenades are being washed and laquered (to prevent rusting).

Tapping (i.e. putting a screw thread into) the filler hole in the body. This factory was in Mill Street West, Aston.

Manufacturing base plugs for the grenades. During the war the allied forces used over 76 million grenades, half of which were made in Birmingham.

Cutting metal blanks which will be pressed into levers for the grenades.

Pressing out the levers from the flat metal blanks.

Reaming the hole for the detonator (i.e. machining it to an exact circle).

74

Drilling the hole for the striker. The levers have now been attached.

The assembly room: strikers being added and the final checks carried out.

A young lad – too young for military service – sorts the scrap metal off-cuts at the end of the production process. These will then be recycled to aid the war effort.

The packing room where crates of grenades are secured with ropes before dispatch. The use of materials such as paper, string, wood and rope for packing explosives, and explosive munitions such as hand grenades, was to prevent possible generation of sparks when they were being moved.

Aerial view of the aircraft factory at Birmingham's Castle Bromwich airfield, *c.* 1943. The airfield was given over to aircraft production during the Second World War, starting with Spitfire fighters in 1940 and followed with Lancaster bombers a year later.

Lancaster fuselage assembly in the factory's B Block, like the rest of this sequence from around 1943.

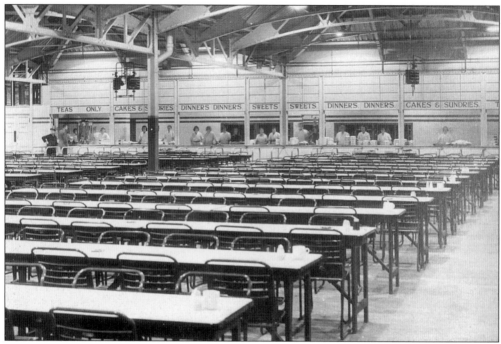

The calm before the storm: the works canteen with staff readying themselves for the next mealtime rush.

A meal in full swing. Such breaks were carefully planned in order to minimise disruption of production.

Leading edge sections for Spitfire wings are manufactured in C Block. Sections of fuselages for the fighters are visible in the distance.

A completed Spitfire on the runway, either undergoing tests or about to be delivered to its squadron.

A hand-made poster, meant as a morale-booster, advertising the factory's Sports & Social Club with some of its activities depicted. (Further illustrations of the factory's wartime role can be found in the *Birmingham Transport* volume in this series.)

Five
Motor City

Birmingham has long been known as Britain's Motor City, with good reason. The car manufacturers Austin and Wolseley both began life here in the 1900s, and, together with ancillary household name suppliers such as Lucas (for electrical components) and Dunlop (for tyres), made the city a major centre for the manufacture of motor vehicles. Covering the history of the industry in a handful of photographs is a daunting task, but it is hoped that those in this section provide an informative overview of what is now a rapidly-dwindling part of Birmingham's industrial heritage.

The first prototype Austin is put through its paces at the new Longbridge factory in April 1906. The car is a 25/30hp, four-cylinder tourer and, including a smaller 15/20hp model, a grand total of twenty-three cars had been sold by that October.

The Austin factory, September 1922. The traffic-free road seems a world away from today's Longbridge.

Inside the factory, c. 1922. This is a production line, or 'track', of the period. Again, the scene is a far cry from the mechanised factory of today.

One of the bodyshops, probably at a slightly later date than the previous photograph. At this time, body parts were still being assembled by hand.

A similar view, at the same date. While rolling chassis lent themselves readily to the track system of assembly, bodies did not until the advent of more complex production lines.

An axle track at Longbridge, *c.* 1930.

An engine shop, 1948. Four-cylinder engines are being assembled in lighter, more modern conditions. Although still primitive in comparison, the production lines are recognisably similar to those of today. Four years later Austin and Morris would amalgamate to form the British Motor Corporation.

The Mini assembly line, *c.* 1963. The model was launched in 1959 as the new Austin Seven and not renamed the Mini until early 1962. Here final adjustments are being made to them before the cars are driven away. By the time production of the model ceased in 2000, an impressive total of 5,287,862 cars had been built.

The 1100/1300 assembly line, *c.* 1963. The 1100 was launched, as a Morris, in August 1962, with the Austin version following a year later. The bodies have not yet been painted.

Painted bodies are stacked for storage until required to receive their engines, axles, wheels, windows and interior fittings, c. 1965.

The Austin Cambridge assembly line, probably around 1959. This was the year production of this model – launched in 1954 – was discontinued, to be replaced by a range of more modern saloons.

Nash Metropolitan bodies about to enter the 'Rota Dip' for treatment, *c*. 1961. The Metropolitan was a collaboration between Austin and the Nash Co. of America, with an Austin engine in a Fisher & Ludlow body (see pp 26-27). During its production period of 1954-1961, some 97,000 models were sold in Britain and the USA.

Assembling Mini and 1100/1300 automatic transmission and engine units, *c*. 1965. Bins for parts to be added to the suspended engines are on the left – compare the scene with that of the earlier engine line pictured on p. 84.

Another great name from Birmingham's car-making past: the first in a sequence depicting the Wolseley Motor Works, around 1926. This aerial view shows the factory site at Adderley Park, now occupied by Duddeston Mill Trading Estate.

Workers coming and going at the Wolseley works – probably changing over shifts – with the entrance gateway in the distance. The man on point duty has little traffic to deal with, as this is a time well before cars became affordable to the people who made them. The company's full title was the Wolseley Tool & Motor Car Co. Ltd.

Assembling chassis on (by today's standards) extremely crude rigs. Originally the Wolseley Sheep Shearing Machine Co., the firm began making cars in 1895 and was taken over by engineering conglomerate Vickers, Sons & Maxim Ltd six years later.

Axle assembly: Lister 'Auto Trucks' were used for moving smaller components around the site, so vast was it.

Manufacturing brake drums. Note the overhead power shafting and belt drives to the machinery.

Marrying chassis with their axles and wheels. The suspension is provided by leaf springs – a direct link back to the motorcar's horse-drawn ancestry.

At the forge in the factory's foundry. The firm's proud boast was that it was the only car maker to make all parts, except tyres, magnetos and accumulators, in its own factory – and mainly from company-produced material!

In the casting shop. In the foreground water, for cooling the long-handled tools used to manipulate the hot metal, is being drawn either from a well or from an underground reservoir.

Women workers. They appear to be cutting-out and stitching trim panels for car interiors.

Their male counterparts work on larger upholstery pieces, probably seat covers.

What appears to be an on-site garage for servicing cars. Hand-propelled trolleys are used to move whole engines around, and lifting tackle running on girders to hoist them into position. The firm went into liquidation in 1926 and was bought by its rival, Morris. (The name was later resurrected, notably on a Mini variant.)

In the works of Fisher & Ludlow again, with a stockpile of stamped-out car body parts: saloon backs and rear wheel arches to the fore, and doors against the far wall, destined for vehicle manufacturers and coachbuilders in Birmingham and elsewhere.

Another world-famous Birmingham name connected with the car industry was that of Joseph Lucas Ltd. This was the dynamo armature production line, probably around 1970. The company's parent factory was in Newtown but it had other works around the city.

In the Lucas factory in Shaftmoor Lane, probably in the 1970s. Vehicle headlamp bodies are being aluminized, as seen through a fish-eye lens.

The Manor Mills Dunlop works in Rocky Lane, Aston, sometime before the firm moved to Fort Dunlop in Erdington in 1916. Although Irish in origin, Dunlop is another name with a long Birmingham – and motor industry – connection.

STAND No. 91.

DUNLOPS

The British tyres that helped to win the 1906 British

TOURIST TROPHY,
GRAPHIC TROPHY,

17 out of the 22 races at Blackpool,

The Schulte Cup (London to Edinburgh and back),

The Scottish Reliability Trials,

The Sunbeam record (John O'Groats to Land's End and back),

Mr. Cecil Edge's non-stop drive of 720 miles,

Also the British and World's Records by Huntley Walker and A. Lee Guinness.

DUNLOP TYRES

are made in England, and both at

Olympia and the Stanley Show
there were more

DUNLOPS

fitted to cars exhibited than

ANY TWO OTHER MAKES COMBINED.

DUNLOP TYRE CO.,
LIMITED,
ASTON, BIRMINGHAM.

A Dunlop Tyre Co. Ltd advertisement from Birmingham's third annual Motor Show held at Bingley Hall from Friday 18 January to Saturday 26 January 1907. Motor shows are by no means as recent a concept as some might think – nor is their connection with Birmingham. Bingley Hall, off Broad Street, may be no more, but a link with the past is maintained with the International Convention Centre being sited there.

Six

Food and Drink

Like any other village or small town, early Birmingham would have been well served by a number of local food and drink manufacturers, principally bakers and brewers – their products being the staple diet of the mass of the people until well into the nineteenth century. (Bread was cheap and nutitious, beer was nutritious and made the local water potable.) As the town grew, so other food manufacturers appeared, supplying markets further afield; perhaps the most famous of these was – and still is – the chocolate manufacturing firm of Cadburys.

Telephone No. 1000 Central.   Telegrams: "SODA, BIRMINGHAM."

The Birmingham Syphon Co., Ltd.,

MERIDEN WELLS,
MERIDEN STREET, BIRMINGHAM.

Mineral Waters of the Highest Quality.

Specialities:

CROWN CORK SODA WATER.   PALE DRY GINGER ALE.
LEMONADE.   QUININE AND STONE BEER.

The above Mineral Waters are on Sale in all Bars of this Theatre.

Believe it or not, Birmingham water was once bottled, as this advertisement for a Digbeth firm shows. It comes from the Theatre Royal's souvenir programme for its 1925-26 pantomime, *Humpty Dumpty*. In fact, many businesses – especially breweries – drew pure water from their own wells and with today's ever-increasing reliance on the mains supply, there is now the possibility is that the water table below the city might rise to a dangerous level.

Duddeston Flour Mill, 1864. When Birmingham was but a small market town, it would have been served by a number of flour mills, powered by water, in the surrounding countryside. All have long since been swallowed up by the encroaching suburbs though one – Sarehole Mill in

Hall Green – has been preserved. (This building dates back to the eighteenth century though there was a mill on the site at least 200 years before that.) The miller at Duddeston in 1864 was Robert Evans; one of his horse-drawn delivery wagons can be seen on the right.

Barnes' bakery on Potter's Hill, Aston, *c.* 1920. This was one of the many shops where the flour from the mills would end up, to be baked on the premises as a range of products during the night and early morning for sale that same day. Note the advertisement for pikelets – a Midlands word, still used, for what are otherwise known as crumpets.

W. Broadbent's sack works in Mill Lane, Deritend, 4 May 1938. Dry goods, such as flour, needed a convenient means of packaging for their transportation, hence the existence of manufactories such as this. Note the display of barrels on the pavement – another part of Broadbent's product range.

More barrels, this time in use on one of Ansell's drays, 1951. Once a common sight around Britain's breweries, these drays have long since been replaced by motor lorries, except for a handful retained for publicity purposes. Ansell's Brewery in Aston closed in 1981, leaving Britain's second-largest city without a single brewery!

A staff photograph at Smith's crisp factory in Tyseley, probably in the 1930s. The savoury snack industry has always been closely allied with the pub trade, but corner shops would have been important customers as well. Those little blue bags of salt in the crisp bags are still remembered fondly by those of a certain age.

101

Richard Cadbury and his wife, 1896. Richard and his brother George took over their father's cocoa business in 1861 and in 1894 established Bournville village, by the new factory (built in 1879) between Selly Oak and Stirchley, to house its workers. The remaining photographs in this chapter give a brief look at the factory he founded, and its workers. He died just three years after this photograph was taken.

Girls packing cocoa, 1912. The dry powder is fed into the hopper on each machine from the pipe above, weighed electrically and the correct amount discharged through a funnel into the waiting canister. Each tin would then be sealed, labelled and packed into boxes for distribution to shops around the country.

Packing chocolates, 1930. The boxes proclaim that these are intended for a limited, 'one-off' market to commemorate the twentieth anniversary of the accession of King George V.

Cadbury's office staff are about to commence their annual road run, 1926. Female participation was of course completely out of the question at that time. Judging by the onlookers' clothes – and the posture of some of the runners – it is certainly not a warm summer's day!

The Cadbury works in Bournville Lane, 1931. The occasion would appear to be a staff outing of some kind – or have the fleet of Midland Red coaches brought visitors to the factory to experience the forerunner of today's Cadbury World?

Part of the production line complex, probably around 1960. The ladies are packing the firm's famous Dairy Milk bars (or 'blocks') as they exit the wrapping machinery. The naked bars on the right would appear to have come through unclothed.

Decorating Easter eggs, again probably around 1960. These are most definitely aimed at the luxury end of this seasonal market, their high cost accounted for by their sheer size and the time required for the intricate hand decoration.

Unloading milk churns at the factory, probably around 1930. Like many large industrial complexes of the time, the factory possessed its own internal railway system. The locomotive is No. 2 *Cadbury* (built around 1896). The railway closed in 1974, its locos and stock replaced by road vehicles.

Bournville Station, *c.* 1910. The occasion is the departure of a Cadbury's Holiday Special, almost certainly taking workers and their families on a day's outing to the seaside. The factory is still served by this mainline railway station, bringing workers to the factory and visitors to the 'chocolate experience' of Cadbury World.

Seven

Fun and Games

Manufacturing in Birmingham has probably always had its lighter side, certainly in terms of some of the goods produced. One of its nationally-known brand names is that of the Chad Valley Co. Ltd, a celebrated manufacturer of all manner of board games, dolls, toys, jigsaws and the like. (The rustic-sounding name was taken from the Chad Brook, a small watercourse in Harborne where the factory was located.) The first fourteen photographs in this section depict scenes in the factory over some twenty years, and show childhood favourites that will be remembered with affection by many.

Painting the white spots on dominoes, *c.* 1950. A set of 'double-six' dominoes, as shown here, contains 28 'tiles' with a total of 168 spots; a set of double-nine dominoes, popular in Northern England, contains 55 tiles with a grand total of 395 spots – all of which had to be painted by hand!

Nailing the wire 'spider' (actually more like a spider's web) onto dart boards before final packing, c. 1950. Judging by the thinness of the boards, which were probably made from a single ribbon of paper tightly wound into a roll or a disc of stiff cork, and the multi-coloured faces, these are destined to be sold as children's playthings, rather than for serious pub or club use.

Assembling and packing novelty crackers, c. 1935. Although very much a seasonal sale item – as were many of the firm's products – their manufacture would have occupied much more of the year than just the Christmas period.

Painting toy cut-out dogs, c. 1935. Note the primitive spray booth being used and the girl's lack of a protective mask, neither of which would be countenanced today.

The painted dogs are gathered after drying on the central heating pipes!

A craftsman cuts out pieces of a children's jigsaw puzzle, c. 1950. The puzzle would have been made from a sheet of plywood onto which had been glued a coloured picture; it takes its name from the foot-powered tool – a jigsaw – that the workman is using.

Part of the jigsaw production line, c. 1935. Express trains were perennially popular subjects while the aeroplanes on the right exemplified the technological wonders of the day.

Girls assembling a simple spelling game, *c.* 1930. The lettered pieces are cut out with jigsaws by the boys on the platform to the right.

An assembly room with a wide range of board games being put into their boxes, *c.* 1950.

More assembly and packing work, *c.* 1950. This time the toys are wooden pull-along Donald Ducks.

Similar toys – including two more Walt Disney favourites, Pluto and Mickey Mouse – are put through their paces for the benefit of the camera, *c.* 1950.

Checking the strings on an earlier example of this type of toy: a horse and jockey, *c.* 1935.

Horse and jockeys again, only this time on a much smaller scale, *c.* 1950. The game is Escalado, with the players' horses having to be wound along to the winning post.

An official Great Western Railway photograph of the packing room at Chad Valley, c. 1935. Chad Valley was responsible for producing the railway company's famous range of jigsaws, now very much collectors' items. Between 1924 and 1937 nearly fifty different puzzles were produced, featuring mainly trains and West Country beauty spots. Most had 150-200 pieces and were sold for 2s 6d, though a few had up to 400 pieces and cost 5s.

The James Watt Street premises of a billiard table manufacturer, Birmingham Billiards Ltd, probably in the late 1950s or early 1960s. The building appears empty and ready for demolition, destined to make way for yet another multi-storey car park.

A party of school children passes the Theatre Royal at No. 102 New Street, *c*. 1902. The upstairs rooms of the theatre's frontage housed the showrooms of Burroughes & Watts Ltd, billiard table manufacturers. At that time billiards enjoyed a popularity equal to that of snooker today. The other major Birmingham manufacturer of the period was Thomas Padmore & Sons of No. 118 Edmund Street. Burroughes & Watts still trade, in Halesowen, and are justly famed for the quality of their cues.

Outdoor sports should not be forgotten: this was the premises of Reuben Heaton & Sons Ltd, fishing reel manufacturers, in 1916. The firm was established in 1857 and occupied the Universal Works at Nos 38 and 40 New Street, Aston (later moving to an industrial estate in Tamworth).

Inside Heaton's factory, 1916. Note the (barely-guarded) circular saw (to be used for shaping the wooden blanks), the half-finished reels hanging from the roof and the assembled reels on the workbench to the right.

Machinery in another of Heaton's workshops, again 1916. Belt drives to the lathes take their power from the overhead shafting, driven by an engine elsewhere in the factory. Whether women traditionally worked in this industry, or whether their employment was a consequence of the war, is not known.

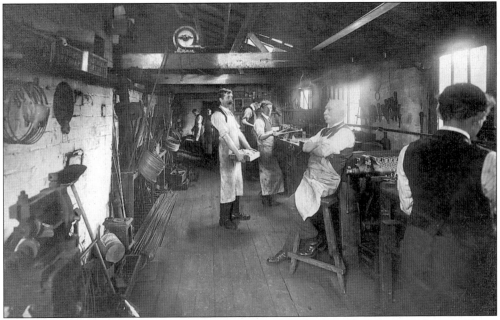

Another part of the Heaton premises, 1916. Hand-crafting, rather than machine-working, would appear to be going on here – by some of the workers, at least! As in the previous photographs, there seems to be a complete absence of artificial light of any kind in the workshops.

Brass Lined SEA REELS.

Since 1926 we have considerably improved the finish. The Mechanical details are, and have been from the start, perfect. A thoroughly hard wearing Reel.

In response to repeated requests from our customers we have decided to market a thoroughly well made CHEAPER RANGE at the undernoted Prices. The value is unapproached by any other make, and EVERY ONE carries our guarantee.

MADE OF BEST GUNSTOCK WALNUT.

Stout Spindles.

Unbreakable

Springs,

PUT IN BY SPECIAL METHOD.

No 28

Stout Wheels.

Pinion Cut.

Special Wear-

Resisting Catches.

9/3	10/-	11/-	12/-	13/6	each.
4	4½	5	5½	6	inches.

With HEATON'S Patent Line Guard, 1/- each extra.

Spindles **Interchangeable** and Spare Spindle supplied, if required, that can be put in in three minutes, or less.

Advertisement from a Heaton catalogue, c. 1930. The firm proudly boasted: 'We probably Make and Sell more Wood and Brass Lined Sea Reels than all the other English Makers put together – and we guarantee every one.'

Eight
The Workshop of the World

To close, a brief look at just some of the other manufacturing industries that fall outside the groupings covered in the previous sections but were once instrumental in earning for Birmingham the nicknames 'Workshop of the World' and 'City of a Thousand Trades'.

Truly the workshop of the world: an official photograph of a visit by His Imperial Highness Prince Tsai Tse and members of the Chinese Special Commission to the Metropolitan Amalgamated Railway Carriage & Wagon Co. Ltd at Saltley, 14 May 1906. The gentleman to the right in the back row, with the white whiskers, is Sir Benjamin Stone, famous photographer and local politician.

Basket-making at Preedy Bros of 16 Heath Mill Lane, off the High Street, Deritend, probably around 1950. This might not be an industry associated with mid-twentieth century central Birmingham, though a clue to its survival lies in its location: a few hundred yards from the city's wholesale markets.

A wheelwright at F. Parr Ltd of Nos 28-30 Dean Street, October 1952. Here axles are sawn to length, halfway through the construction of a small wooden wheel. This might seem another unlikely Birmingham industry at so late a date but the firm's location right by the wholesale markets – with all their attendant carts and barrows – is the giveaway.

Still at Parr's, October 1952. Here one of the wooden felloes which make up the rim of a larger wheel is being shaped by hand with a spokeshave. The 1952 *Kelly's Directory* of Birmingham describes the firm as 'manufacturers of wooden & steel wheelbarrows, trucks &c.'

Parr's again, October 1952. An iron tyre is being forced onto a wheel rim. The smoke comes from wood burning: the tyre is heated beforehand to make it expand so when it cools and contracts it binds the constituent parts of the wheel together in – literally a grip of iron. A smaller band has been placed round the end of the hub (or 'nave') in order to protect it.

Haynes' rope walk in Hockley, 1900. The sign proclaims the owner to be Richard Haynes, rope and twine maker – possibly the man on horseback. On the left is the edge of the grounds of Thornhill House, built for Matthew Boulton's daughter and demolished in 1900; in the distance is Soho Road railway station.

The rope walk again, 1900. Close by the railway station, a boy is spinning out fibres from the bag around the man's waist, the latter person expertly controlling the process after years of experience. The result will be a thick thread which will then be twisted together with others, in the rope walk, to make string and twine; these in turn might be wound into ropes. The business closed around 1914, after the death of Haynes.

The premises of G.E. Mewis Ltd at No. 13 St Paul's Square, 1956. Here too ropes were made, this time in an urban setting in the yard behind. A neighbouring building in this short street, just off the picture to the left, was converted a few years ago into a pub, appropriately named The Rope Walk.

St Paul's Square again, this time in 1941. G.E. Mewis Ltd had another manufactory in the square, occupying this building on the corner of Caroline Street where cords for sash windows were produced. Both the firm's premises have been given a new lease of life as offices with the general 'smartening-up' of this part of the city centre.

The Saltley premises of Smith, Stone & Knight's paper mills, 1895. These men are operating a calender – a machine for smoothing a finish onto rolls of paper or card.

Inside the Saltley paper mills again, 1895. Here women pack card sheets for dispatch, under the watchful eye of a male supervisor.

Nos 64-65 Hampton Street, 1901. The workshops and salerooms of W. Complin, wholesale and retail cabinet maker and upholsterer – typical small business premises on the fringes of the city in late-Victorian and early-Edwardian days.

A maker's plate for the Birmingham Safe Co. of No. 44 Coleshill Street. Such plates, a few inches in diameter and usually made of brass, were fixed to the fronts of safes to advertise their makers. They are now collector's items. This particular example appears to be from a model named after James W. Burnside, the firm's proprietor. In 1910 some twenty safe manufacturers were listed as having premises in the city.

At the General Electric Co. Ltd's switchgear works in Witton, 20 April 1966. Here motor control centres are being checked before they are shipped out to the Durgapur steelworks in West Bengal.

At the GEC's Witton works, 4 August 1966. This is a Witton-Kramer 55in diameter electric lifting magnet, raising 2,450lbs of pig-iron during a load test. Officially described as 'lightweight', it weighed 3,800lbs.

At the GEC again. Birmingham is renowned as a producer of electrical equipment of all shapes and sizes – from the smallest motorcar component to the biggest dynamo armature such as this.

Women pack bunting at J.T. Darlington Ltd of Birches Green Works, Spring Lane in 1953. Presumably this was a sideline to the firm's principal business as a timber merchant and, given the date, it seems probable that the coronation of Queen Elizabeth II is about to be celebrated. Will the next coronation be the occasion of as much festivity as the last one?

In contrast, a sombre note upon which to end: the new Yardley Road premises of John White & Sons, monumental sculptors. The firm had just expanded from its original premises on the corner of Yardley Road and Mansfield Road in South Yardley and by 1910 had a third outlet at No. 9 Soho Hill, Handsworth – business was obviously booming!